CW01021065

Business Plan Template
How to Write a Business Plan

Chris Gattis

www.BusinessStartup101.com

Business Plan Template

Chris Gattis

www.BusinessStartup101.com

Copyright ©2010 by Christopher G. Gattis

All rights reserved.

Published by Blue Point Publishers, a division of Blue Point Strategies, LLC, Huntsville, Alabama.

No part of this publication may be reproduced, stored in a retrieval system, or transmitted in any form or by any means, electronic, mechanical, photocopying, recording, scanning, or otherwise, except as permitted under Section 107 and 108 of the 1976 United States Copyright Act, without the prior written permission of the Publisher. Requests to the publisher for permission should be addressed to the Permission Department, Blue Point Publishing at books@bluepointstrategies.com.

Limit of Liability/Disclaimer of Warranty: While the publisher and author have used their best efforts in preparing this book, they make no representation or warranties with respect to the accuracy or completeness of the contents of this book and specifically disclaim any implied warranties of merchantability or fitness for a particular purpose. No warranty may be created or extended by sales representatives or written sales materials. The advice and strategies contained herein may not be suitable for your situation. You should consult with a professional where appropriate. Neither the publisher nor author shall be liable for any loss of profit or any other commercial damages, including but not limited to special, incidental, consequential, or other damages.

For information on discounts for bulk purchases and our other products, please contact Blue Point Publishers at books@bluepointstrategies.com.

ISBN-13: 9781466424227
ISBN-10: 1466424222

Printed in the United States of America

Table of Contents

1 Introduction

One of the most difficult projects for new business owners seems to be writing a business plan. The process is really quite straightforward, but it causes many sleepless nights and nervous days for would-be entrepreneurs. Writing a business plan can be broken down into subparts, making the job a more reasonable mountain to climb. And while new research done at the University of Maryland's business school suggests that venture capitalists no longer read business plans, but instead rely almost entirely on their 'gut feeling', you should still give this project your best effort. Most new business owners will not be presenting their idea to venture capitalists in the first place, and those that will, need all the practice they can get.

The business plan document represents a summary of your plans, research and expected performance of your business. It is presented in a format that makes for easy reading for bankers and other outsiders. The business plan is just a summary of what you've learned about the industry, competition, customer and your plan to make a profit. It's really no more complicated than that. At this point in the process you should have already done the research and made many of the important decisions. Now it's time to write them down.

How detailed your writing style will depend on your business. If you're a small business with only meager cash needs, you can probably get away with simple paragraphs and bulleted lists for most items. If your business is complicated and requires significant funding, you'll need a sharper pencil. You don't have to be a published author to write a business plan. Only the most complicated businesses and those with significant cash needs should have a lengthy plan. Most businesses can get by with a short business plan write-up supplemented with supporting documentation and financials.

Business Plan Template

2 Types of Business Plans

While there are as many types of business plans as there are types of businesses, I generally break down business plan types into three categories: Formal, Informal and Summary.

Formal

A formal business plan is what most entrepreneurs think of as a business plan. It is the most comprehensive and detailed form of your plan. The purpose of the formal plan is for presentation to bankers, investors or other partners of the business. While all business plans are summaries of the research, conclusions, goals and objectives, the formal plan gives the most detail. These individuals will need the detailed analysis of the industry, competition, customer and SWOT analysis as well as financial projections. The analysis will typically be presented as a narrative with the addition of charts, graphs and tables to help illustrate the data where appropriate.

Informal

An informal business plan summarizes the same research, conclusions, goals and objectives as the formal plan, but in a more summarized fashion. This type plan is typically used for the management team to guide planning and budgeting and lead the performance measurement thinking of this group. This type of plan is more generally thought of as a strategic plan. It will give lots of details in the marketing and promotion areas as well as in operational details that speak to changes in operations or manufacturing.

The management team was most likely involved in the preparation of the plan and doesn't need the detail on who the corporate attorney is and what type of bookkeeping system is in place. They need the appropriate detail in the strategic sections of the overall plan.

The informal plan will also not have a big financial projections section. Since this plan is primarily designed for the management of the company, it will contain budgets and cost projections only. The management will continually update the group with 'live' financials to reflect the actual operations of the business. These actual financials can then be compared to the budgets and projections.

Summary

The summary business plan is typically used for marketing purposes where detailed information about the company would not be appropriate. It might be used as a recruitment tool for potential employees or to give vendors and other business partners an indication of the overall goals and plans of the company. Confidential and proprietary information will not be included in this type of plan.

Many times a summary plan will be used as a recruitment tool at a job fair or other event where employers and prospective employees will interact.

The type of plan you use will depend on the situation and the audience. It is important to understand though, that the research, conclusions, goals and objectives are completed before writing the plan and do not change based on the type of plan you write. The proper research and planning is necessary to run a successful operation and doesn't change based on your plan type. We will focus on the formal plan in this book.

3 The Business Planning Process

One key point before we start: don't confuse your business plan document with the business planning process. Too many hopeful entrepreneurs think that if they do the work and research necessary to write a business plan, then that's it. Keep in mind that a business plan is a summary of all your planning and research. There's really no substitute for doing your research.

The business planning process should include the following steps:

Step #1

Develop your business model. Define the process by which your business will operate and provide products or services to the market. What partners will you use? Where will you be located? What resources will you need?

Step #2

Develop your marketing plan. This is a big piece. It starts with understanding your customer, your industry and your competitors. It includes developing a strategy for interacting with your customers and using the industry trends to your advantage. It includes developing distribution channels and a promotion and pricing plan. It includes understanding how your competition operates in the marketplace and how your strengths and weaknesses can be leveraged against the opportunities and threats of that marketplace. It's way more than just creating a Facebook page.

Step #3

Make your revenue projections. This is the single hardest part of the whole process. If I create a business that looks and operates like this and uses a marketing plan like that, how many widgets can I expect to sell? Unfortunately, this is a question that I can't answer for you. You'll have to base it on your research and your discussions with other business owners and mentors. Finally, you've got to make a prediction: how many units of product or service can you sell if everything goes according to plan?

Step #4

Use the *Three Tools of Financial Viability* ™ **to test your business model.** In my book *Business Start-up 101: From Great Idea to Profit...Quick!* I identify three tools that every entrepreneur should know and come to love. These tools are 1) the income statement projection, 2) the cash flow report, and 3) the break-even analysis. These are the tools that will help you sleep at night. These are the tools that will help you decide if this crazy business model is a keeper or a harebrained idea. In fact, if you approach the analysis of your plan in a conservative and honest way based on actual market forces, and use the three tools, you'll have a good idea if your business idea should be launched or not. The tools will give you a factual basis for making business decisions. And isn't that the big hang-up for most people? If you only had confidence that your idea would work or not, you would get started. The *Three Tools of Financial Viability* ™ will give you that confidence.

You can get a copy of *Business Start-up 101: From Great Idea to Profit...Quick!* from www.BusinessStartup101.com or Amazon.

Step #5

Rinse and repeat. What if I don't like the outcome I get from using the tools? Frankly, I'd be surprised if you did get the outcome you hoped for in the first iteration of your plan. The whole idea of the tools is one of modification. The tools are tools; you use them to shape your plan and turn it into something you can love. Start with the income statement. If you don't like the results you predict in your income statement, go back and make changes to your business model that will give you a different income statement outcome. DO NOT tweak your income statement so that it says what you want it to say. These tools will help you fix your model so that you are rewarded with a plan that works. Don't fall into the trap of so many others who think the income statement is for the banker and they need not be concerned with its projections. This is your business and you are the one who will suffer most if you cheat. You're really cheating yourself.

After making as many changes to your business model as is necessary to give you an income statement that meets your goals, move on to the cash flow. Run the cash flow based on the income statement. Determine if your business model generates enough cash or whether you have enough resources to fund the cash needs of your business. If not, go back to your business model and start the whole process over. Once you are happy with the income statement and the cash flow, move on to the break-even analysis (for anything other than a service business). If you like the results and think that they are reasonable then move on, if not, it's back to the beginning. Continue this process through as many iterations as necessary until you get results that meet your needs.

If you can't tweak your business model enough to get financial statement results that meet your needs, then your idea s probably not viable. What's *viable*? Viable means that real people will pay real money in sufficient quantity to meet your needs. So if you plan is not viable, then your business idea doesn't make sense. If, after all of your iterations, you like the results of your financial statements, move on the Step #6.

Step #6

Write your business plan. Only now can you write your business plan. Many people that I coach can't understand why writing a business plan is so hard. When I inquire about their research, it becomes evident that it hasn't been done. How could you expect to write a summary of a business planning process, if you haven't gone through the business planning process? If you don't do the research and make the plans and crunch the numbers, you have nothing to summarize. Do the business planning and the business plan is easy.

4 The Business Plan Template

If you have no idea what a business plan should look like or how it's written, and are really nervous about writing one, then conduct a quick search of the Internet for examples of business plans. There are some excellent examples of business plans in hundreds of locations easily found with a search. You should be able to locate sample plans for businesses similar to yours to see layouts, templates (although you'll get that here!) and styles. You will also see what type of language is typically used and what details are included. There is no reason to be nervous. Just address the topics in this template that are appropriate for your business (not all of them will apply to your business) plus anything else that you lender wants, and you'll be fine.

17

One of the most common questions I get asked by clients and in coaching appointments is how many pages a business plan should contain. The real answer is 'as many as it takes.' The answer you want depends on the size of business enterprise you are starting. If you're starting a very small business, you should be able to convey the essence of your plan in 8 to at most 15 pages, plus financials and addenda. If you're starting a big business or needs lots of money from banks or investors, then your plan may be more like 20 – 50 pages, plus financials and addenda. Remember, the weight of your plan is not what's important. In fact, if you submit a 50 page plan to either a banker or investor, I can almost guarantee that it will not be read completely. If you can't say what you need to say in fewer pages than that, then you better be starting a huge business or have someone help you cut it down. The idea is to get the recipient to actually read and be convinced to approve your request, not use it to line their bid cage.

Another common question concerns which tools to use to create the plan. The main options are a word processing program versus business plan software. If you don't have MS Word or other similar word processing program, you can utilize Open Office open source productivity software. It functions similarly to MS Office and is free. It includes applications for word processing, spreadsheets and graphics. If you need to make presentations, it also includes that application as well as other useful business applications. Any basic word processing program that will allow you to write text and insert images will work. For your financial projections, you'll need a spreadsheet application that will generate charts to summarize your data and projections. That's really all you need. There is no need to buy software or subscribe to any service.

For some people, only a software template will do. There is business plan software in a range of prices from $19.95 and up. However, you don't need software or a fancy plan document. You can use my example format as a starting point or any of the ones you find on the Internet. The important thing is that you cover the items that are important to your business. No software or template can tell you that. Even I can't tell you that without knowing details about your business operations and funding needs. With that said, here's a sample table of contents that you can use as a starting point.

Executive Summary

Organization

Industry & Markets

Marketing Plan

Financial Analysis & Projected Financials

Addenda

A detailed business plan template follows with many of the items listed for a generic business. If you choose to use this format, add any additional items that are required for your business and delete the ones that don't apply. The list that follows is a suggested starting point. You should modify it as needed to tell the story of your business. Try to tell your story from the reader's perspective. If you were reading a business plan about your business, what would you want to know? We'll look at each of these six basic categories in detail in the coming pages.

5 Executive Summary

The first page of your business plan is the executive summary; you should write it last.

The executive summary is a one-page summary of your plan. It should include a brief summary of the four main sections of your plan: Organization, Industry & Markets, Marketing Plan and Financials. Finally, it should include a statement of your financial need. That is, how much money do you need and how do you plan to repay that money. Many readers will only read this page and skip ahead to the financial statements. Take a little time to get this page right. You have to condense your whole business plan down into a page or at most, two pages. If you have only one page to make or break your business plan, what would you say?

Resist the temptation to give the reader the whole story in the executive summary. This is a place for brevity. State the problem and how your business model will solve the problem. Tell how your business is unique, how you will solve industry problems and make your customers love you, and how you are uniquely qualified to lead such a business. Write about the resources you will put into place with the cash you are asking for and how it will be used to create a profitable business.

The executive summary is very simple. However, its simplicity is what makes it so difficult. Again, spend plenty of time getting this part right.

6 Business Organization

This section will tell your readers who you are, what you'll make and who will do the making. You will want to include at least a sentence about the topics listed including legal structure. You may want to include information about how you will account for the business (i.e. accounting software, MS Excel or shoe box), if you're using an accounting firm, attorney, insurance broker and so forth.

Ownership information should be included in your business plan including the names of owners, their ownership interest and proposed involvement in the business. Do they have any expertise in a business like the one you are proposing? In addition, you'll want to include a section on the management of your business. Who are the individuals and what is their

expertise? How will these individuals help you achieve success?
If you have a board of directors or an advisory board, discuss
their specific skills and how they will help you.

This portion of the business plan is very straightforward and
can be completed quickly. At this point, you should already
know all this information. Following is a minimum list of topics
that should be covered in this section:

Description of Business
Products & Services
Location(s)
Owners & Principals
Board of Directors/Board of Advisors
Organization Chart
Legal Structure
Employee Recruitment & Retention
Recordkeeping
Professional Relationships
    Attorney
    Banker
    CPA/Accountant
    Insurance Agent
    Consultant
    Other Professional Advisor(s)

Description of Business – Describe the business model in broad terms. How will you make products or deliver services. Why will customers choose to do business with you instead of your competition?

Products & Services – Describe the specific products and services that will be delivered by your company. How do these products or services compare to those already on the market?

Location – Where is the business located and is this important to the sales function? If so, how did you determine which location to select? Include a regional and/or local street map to identify your business and any important geographical points in relation to your business address. You might also include pictures of the exterior and interior of your facility.

Owners & Principals – Describe the owners and a brief overview of their background. You'll likely include a complete resume in the addenda section, so just hit the highlights, concentrating on previous jobs or activities that are especially pertinent to this business. Make sure to identify how these individuals are qualified to run a business like this.

Board of Directors or Advisory Board – Corporations require a board of directors, other forms of legal entity may not. Discuss your board members and/or advisory board not previously discussed and what they bring to the new business.

Organization Chart – Include an organization chart for your business. Even if many or most of the boxes have your name, it shows the reader that you understand how the organization will need to be structured in order to grow and meet its objectives.

Legal Structure – Describe the legal entity (Corporation, LLC, Partnership, Sole Proprietorship, etc.) and why you chose that particular form.

Employee Recruitment & Retention – How will you recruit new employees from companies with existing operations and established benefit plans? In many markets, hiring the right employees can be difficult. You can always hire bodies, but if your business depends on high-quality people, tell the reader how you'll hire the right ones and then keep them once they are on board.

Recordkeeping - How will you account for the operations of your business? Most companies use some sort of accounting software, what will you use?

Professional Relationships – If you've selected the appropriate professionals (and you should have), who are they? A list of professional firms with which you'll depend for advice and counsel, the contact person and location will suffice. This list might include the following professionals:

Attorney

Banker

CPA/Accountant

Insurance Agent

Consultant

Other Professional Advisor(s)

7 Industry & Markets

Market Analysis

The market analysis gets into the meat of your business plan. The market analysis section should reflect your understanding of the market in which you plan to operate. You should include data in this section about the size of the market, its growth expectations, trends, technology developments and so forth.

Within the overall market, what are the different industries? How much volume and in what parts of the world, country or state do they come into play? Understanding the size and trends in your specific industry is crucial to your success. How much of your industry's total volume do you plan to take? What percentage of the total will you represent?

Who is your competition? What is their market share?
What do they do well? What do they do poorly? To the extent
that you know or can find through research, I like to identify
strengths and weaknesses on each major competitor. This sort
of thinking can help you fine-tune your product or service
offering to take advantage of a niche that may not be adequately
covered by your competitors. You need to understand what
products and services your competitors offer and at what price.
It is difficult to get all this type of info on your competitors,
especially if they are small businesses without any public filings.
However, the more information you can get on the strengths and
weaknesses of your competition the better you will be able to
identify opportunities and threats to your business.

Strategic Analysis

The strategic analysis should center on your company
S.W.O.T. analysis. Like in the previous section where you did a
simple strengths and weaknesses analysis on your competitors,
you should do a detailed and thorough analysis of your business.
On what basis do you plan to compete with the other companies
already offering the same product or service in the market? Is
your product or service new? Have you developed a new way of
approaching an old problem? If you're using mentors or
advisors, this would be a good time to have them do a reality
check.

Think you don't have any competitors? Think again! I've never seen a start-up yet without any competition. Sometimes competition comes from unusual sources, like an existing company in another industry or business that springs to life when they see a market opportunity. Sometimes competition comes from the Internet in the form of an on-line company with no physical presence in your market. Whether from a direct, indirect or purely on-line source, every business has competition.

Below is a list of potential discussion items followed by a discussion of each item.

Industry
    Description of Industry
    Industry Trends
    Market Segment(s)
        Detailed Description of Your Market Segment
        Special Market Segment Considerations   Laws & Rules Applying to Your Industry
    Special Industry Considerations
        Capital Restraints
        Environmental Issues
        Ease/Difficulty of Entering Industry
    Brief Description of Major Market

Competition

List Competition (Direct & Indirect)
Brief Description of Direct Competitors
 Company Name & Locations
 Description of Product or Service
 Strengths & Weaknesses
People
Capital
Technology
Intellectual Property
Market Position
History
Location

Customers

Who Are They?
Where Do They Live & Work?
Where Do They Play?
How Much $ Do They Make?
Define Using WHATEVER Socio-Demo-Geo-Characteristic Is Important

Company

S.W.O.T. Analysis (Strengths, Weaknesses, Opportunities & Threats)
Company Profile/Competition/Market
 Employees
 Capital
 Technology
 Intellectual Property
 Market Position
 History
 Location

Let's look at each part of the industry and markets section of your business plan in detail.

Industry

Description of Industry: Describe the general industry in which your business will operate. Define the market in terms of annual dollar volume, geographical boundaries and other market boundaries as such as they exist. Discuss the different market segments or sub-segments that exist and give a brief overview of each major segment.

Industry Trends: What are the major trends in your industry? Most businesses and industries ebb and flow over time as trends change and how business is conducted changes. How is technology affecting your business? Has the state of the economy had any impacts on how business is done or how many players are exiting or entering the industry?

Market Segment(s): Define the market segment or segments in which your business will operate. Give a detailed account of this segment, how it operates, distribution channels, financial considerations, standard payment terms and so forth.

Laws & Rules Applying to Your Industry: Are there any special or unusual laws or regulatory rules that apply to your industry?

Many industries have such rules that affect how business is conducted or that guide how customer relations are managed.

Special Industry Considerations: Are there any other special considerations for your industry? Does the industry have any special capital considerations or environmental concerns? How easy or difficult is it to enter the market? Discuss any special considerations for your company in this section.

Competition

List Competition: Every company in every industry that I've ever seen or contemplated has competition. I occasionally get challenged on this in workshops and classes. However, I have never failed to identify a competitor, either direct or indirect, for any business opportunity. I'm guessing that your business has competition too. Your banker or investor knows this as well, so don't disrespect them by pretending otherwise. Even if you honestly believe that you have no competition, there are companies who could easily enter the market if they thought it interesting.

Brief Description of Competitors: Make a list of your direct and indirect competitors and do a quick analysis of each. Include at a minimum their company name and location and a brief description of their product or services. To the extent that you can get the information, compile a list of the strengths and weaknesses of each competitor. Include a discussion of such items as their employees, financial capability, technologies, intellectual property, history and position in the market. Include any item that is pertinent to their competitive situation or perception in the market.

If geographical considerations are appropriate for your industry or market segment, include a local, regional or other map and identify the location of your business and each major competitor. A simple map is sometimes helpful to the reader in understanding how your location differences affect business performance.

Customers

In the customers section, you want to define who you think your customers are, where they are located, where they live, work and play. You will evaluate your customer profile differently depending of if you will do business in a B2B (business-to-business) environment or a B2C (business-to-consumer) environment, or a combination of the two. Use whatever socioeconomic, demographic and geographic characteristic is important for your business. The more specifically you can identify your customer, the easier it is to target them within your marketing plan.

Use charts, tables, grids, maps, U.S. Census data and any other tool you need to convey this information to the reader.

Company

S.W.O.T. Analysis: A SWOT Analysis is a strategic tool for evaluating the strengths and weaknesses of your company compared to the opportunities and threats within the market. The goal of a SWOT analysis is to identify the key internal and external factors that drive the success of your business. By leveraging your strengths against the opportunities in the market, you can take advantages of developing trends and be in a position to strike when the time is right in the market. In contrast, by analyzing your weaknesses and developing improvement plans, you can stay away from areas where you don't have a competitive advantage in the market place or where the demand will weaken or the obstacles to success are too high.

A SWOT Analysis is usually displayed in a two by two grid with strengths (top) and weaknesses (bottom) along the left and opportunities (top) and threats (bottom) along the right. Feel free to use this type of display, but it's really not necessary. The key is actually doing the thinking about the specific parts of your business and how they rank and then how you'll use that information to take advantage of what the market has to offer.

Don't be surprised to find that many items on the list are actually opposite sides of the same coin. For example, your company may have the latest piece of high-tech, which allows you to get products to market quickly. Such a technology would certainly be considered a strength. However, that technology may be very expensive and have a big financial impact on your monthly cash flow, which is a weakness.

Company Profile: Think about the pieces that make up your company. Your employees, capital, technology, intellectual property, market position, financial position, company history, location, and reputation all have an impact on how you do business. Analyze these type characteristics with the SWOT Analysis in mind. If something is a strength, how can you use it to your advantage? If an item is a weakness, what can you do to improve it over time?

Competition: Where does your competition stack up in this same SWOT Analysis? Consider the same characteristics with which you measured your company.

Market: Based on the competition, the competitive environment and market trends, where are the opportunities and threats in the market? Match your strengths against the opportunities to leverage your position in the market. What opportunities are present that you could leverage if only one of your weaknesses was a strength? Can you improve that characteristic to take advantage of the opportunity? Likewise, what are the threats in the market and how can you position your company to be ready to deal with these realities, or can you create systems, develop technology or training programs to allow your company to remain unaffected by the threats or at least minimize the effects.

Spend a much time as is necessary to complete this analysis and list the salient points in your business plan. The SWOT Analysis will be the basis for all your marketing and promotion plans. It's important to get it right.

8 Marketing Plan

The marketing plan brings together all the research, discussion, pondering and calculating that you've done and uses that information to promote your business brand and your products and services in such a way that your target customers know about your business offerings and are compelled to buy your products and services. If you do this right and follow-up by delivering products and services that exceed your customers expectations, you'll build a loyal following that will reward you with a thriving, growing business.

For most small business start-ups, marketing is some sort of 'black magic' that isn't really understood. Most hopeful entrepreneurs that I coach think they don't understand marketing at all. I'm not suggesting that developing a creative marketing plan is simple. But it's more about doing your research and laying out a logical plan based on that research than it is 'black magic' wizardry.

Keep in mind that you'll develop a separate plan for each market segment. You'll need to approach each segment and target customer with a unique strategy. While some or possibly all parts will be the same, you should assume that all parts will be different for each market segment. After you get all the pieces laid out, you can combine and overlap where it makes sense to take best advantage of your available budget.

Like in the other sections, I'll lay out the template and then discuss it in detail.

Market Situation Analysis
Market Segment(s)
    Target Customer Groups
    Unique Value Proposition
Marketing Strategy
    Product
    Price
    Place
    Promotion
        Goals (Market Objectives)
        Budget

Timetable

Resources Needed

Action Plan/Implementation Tactics

Advertising & Promotion

PR Campaigns

Networking

Monitor/Measure/Test

Much, if not all of your research work should have been completed and summarized in the Industry & Markets section of your business plan. The marketing plan takes that information and creates an actionable plan.

Market Situation Analysis: This is a brief restatement of the market conditions, trends and major opportunities and threats.

Define the Market Segments: Define the target market that this plan will address. You will be developing a specific marketing plan for each target market.

Target Customer Groups: Identify the target customer as specifically as possible.

Unique Value Proposition: This is sometimes called a Unique Selling Proposition. Why would your target customer buy from you instead of the company down the street offering the same product or service? In other words, why is your company so special? Remember, it's all about the customer.

Marketing Strategy: Your marketing strategy will be defined in terms of the 4 P's of Marketing, Product, Price, Place (Distribution) and Promotion.

Product: What product or product line will you promote to this target customer and how does the customer use your product? How does your product solve the target customer's problem or make their life better?

Price: Discuss your pricing strategy for your product line. Will you price higher or lower than your competition? What are the advantages of your pricing strategy relative to your brand and service level? Include list price, discounts, payment terms and any other financial terms like leasing or financing options.

Place (Distribution): How will you get your product to the customer? The distribution channel you use will have a major impact on the pricing and promotion of the product. Will you use one channel exclusively (i.e. retail, direct, distribution, manufacturers rep) or some combination?

Promotion: The promotion plan will be defined by outlining your goals or market objectives, budget, timetable and resources necessary to implement the promotion of your products.

Goals (Market Objectives): What are your promotion goals? Do you want to sell a certain dollar amount or number of products or command a certain percentage of the total market?

Budget: What's your budget for this piece of the marketing plan? Don't forget to include any R&D that might be necessary to get a product ready for market.

Timetable: Over what time do you hope to accomplish your goals?

Resources Needed: What resources are necessary to meet these goals? You have already defined the cash requirement, but what about employees, product samples, equipment run time, special packaging needs and so forth?

Action Plan/Implementation Tactics: What, specifically, are you going to do? Let's look at the specifics of the implementation tactics necessary to promote your products.

Advertising & Promotion: How will you advertise your product? Will you use media such as TV, radio, news papers, magazines, trade journals and billboards? Or will you use internet marketing, email campaigns or pay-per-click advertising?

PR Campaigns: Will you use new conferences, YouTube videos, press releases and industry websites news to promote your product and/or company launch? There are many different definitions of advertising and PR. Use this simple definition: advertising is bought, PR is free.

Networking: Networking can be an effective tool for small business marketing. It can take the form of chamber of commerce 'after hours' or breakfast events or a more formal networking like BNI (Business Networking International). While many of these options do not have a direct cost, they do take time, something which may be in shorter supply than actual cash money.

Monitor/Measure/Test: One of the most important pieces of your marketing plan is the measurement. If you have set goals and objective for your plans, you'll be able to measure the results. If you aren't getting the results you wanted, make changes to your plan. Describe how you will monitor the plans and measure your results.

9 Financial Analysis

In the financial analysis section, you'll want to prove your business idea with financial statements, discuss your need for funds and how you'll repay those funds. You will also need to discuss the assumptions that go into your financial statements. I generally break up the financial section into two parts. I'll give you the list first, and then discuss the parts.

Part 1: Financial Background

Sales Goals & Projections
Resources Needed
 Capital Equipment
 Start-Up Costs
 Marketing Collateral
 Product Samples
 Technology
 Employees
Summary of Financial Need
Financial Statement Assumptions

Part 2: Financials

Summary Charts
Income Statement
Cash Flow Report
Balance Sheet
Break-Even Analysis
Industry Norms & Ratio Analysis

Financial Background

In this section, you'll discuss the goals and needs of your new business. Let's look at each item individually.

Sales Goals & Projections: Based on all your research and planning, how much of your products and services do you expect to sell? I recommend using a table or matrix format to list your total revenue projections. If these projections warrant any discussion, then have it follow the projections.

Resources Needed: You will need certain things to start your business. In some cases it might be manufacturing or fabrication equipment, it might be software, computers or other technology. Marketing collateral, product samples and up-front employee expenses are also frequent resources needed in a start-up operation. Almost every business will have start-up costs associated with beginning operations. Group these expenses into logical categories and sum the costs. Simple lists will be sufficient. If any of the items warrants additional discussion, add it here.

Summary of Financial Need: This item is all about your bank or investor request. Discuss what you need, why you need that amount, your preferred terms and how you intend to repay the money.

Financial Statement Assumptions: As you build your financial statements, make a list of assumptions as you go. This should be a bullet list of all the parts of your financials. For example, if you plan to hire 3 part-time employees in the second month at $12.45 per hour without benefits, say so. Go down the revenue and expense items in the income statement and cash flow and the assets and liabilities of the balance sheet and discuss how you arrived at each figure. You want the reader to have the information at hand if they have questions. You don't want your banker to call and ask where you got the $539 per month for equipment leasing. You want that information included in the plan. This is a really easy step, it's just a list of costs explained or detailed, and it dramatically increases your credibility with the lender or investor.

Financials

This is, as stated earlier, an important piece of your business plan. Many readers will flip to this section after reading the executive summary. Take your time and double check all your figures. Make sure that your assumption figures match your financial statements. Your revenue projections should match your income statement.

Creating income statement projections and cash flow reports is not that difficult. You should be able to complete that financial task. If you can't create a simple income statement and cash flow projection, you may need to take a step back and get some financial education or at least some help before moving forward. You don't have to be an accountant or CPA to start a business, but you do need to understand how to create and understand a basic income statement and know the difference between income and cash flow. I devote many pages to the creation of these two statements in my book *Business Start-up 101: From Great Idea to Profit...Quick!* If you need a primer on basic financial statements, get and read that book or some other financial education. You can get the book at www.BusinessStartup101.com or Amazon.

You will need an income statement projection and cash flow report at a minimum for your start-up business. If you expect massive revenue growth or will require a big loan and lots of capital equipment, then you'll also need a balance sheet. If you are not an accountant or trained in accounting, you'll probably need some help with the balance sheet. If you are not an accountant or trained in accounting, you'll probably need some help with the balance sheet. This is a fairly complicated statement and not one that a first-time entrepreneur could likely create without help. And unlike the income statement and cash flow report, you can start a business just fine without knowing how to create a balance sheet.

If you have an existing business and plan investment in new equipment or infrastructure, you'll need to explain how the investment will be made and what you expect to get in return and under what time frame. A return on investment analysis or ROI will calculate the percentage return you expect to achieve from the investment.

For most business types, I like to start with summary information in the form of charts and graphs that are quick and easy to understand and reflect in picture format, the performance of your business. Follow the charts with the detailed statements. Let's look at the individual items.

Summary Charts: Create charts and graphs that represent your summary and detailed information. At a minimum, have a summary chart for five-year revenue projections as well as an additional chart showing net sales, expenses, and net income before taxes. Also have a cash flow chart showing the monthly cash flow by year. Also have a cash flow chart showing the monthly cash flow by year. You can stack all the years onto one chart as long as the lines can be easily read.

Income Statement: You should create income statement projections for a minimum of two years by month. I really prefer three years worth of detailed statements. If your business will have an especially long break-even period, then additional years may be required. In addition, I would create summary statements going out five years. If you have created detailed statements for that period, then also include a summary by year and include those figures. Use this data to create your income and expense summary chart.

Your income statements should reflect a period equal to your accounting year. For example, if your financial year end is December 31st, your income statements should show months January through December. If you will use a September 30th year end, then your income statements will show October through September. Don't worry if your first few months are blank. Show your business starting in whatever month it will start and also show your start-up costs in the appropriate month before your operations begin. The income statement should reflect how you'll really start and operate.

Cash Flow Report: Create a cash flow report by month that matches each of your income statement projections. Also create a summary five-year report to match the similar income statement.

Balance Sheet: Project, or have your accountant help you project a year-ending balance sheet for each year of your income statement projections.

Break-Even Analysis: If appropriate, complete a break-even calculation and discuss the ramifications. The important part of the break-even is how many units of production are required to achieve a break-even profitability and is selling that many units reasonable, based on the market conditions. The calculation is simple, follow up the calculation with a discussion on the analysis.

Industry Norms & Ratio Analysis: For small start-ups, this probably is not necessary, but it sure is an added bonus. Go to your accountant or regional college or university library and get the industry financial norms for your NAICS code. The information is contained in the *Annual Statement Studies* is published by the Risk Management Association The data comes from actual financial statements from your industry groups by NAICS code. The data is further grouped by both asset size and sales volume. Use the appropriate category and compare your financial projections with the latest year's industry norms. A complete guide to small business financial ratios can be found in my book *Business Start-up 101.*

10 Addenda

The addenda section will vary depending on the reader and their requirements. If you're preparing the business plan for a lender, they will likely have specific requirements for this section. Some common information might include resumes of your key management and owners as well as personal financial statements of the owners. You'll also need to include copies of important legal documents about your business and IRS registration documents showing your federal corporate taxpayer ID number. Any other information that may be helpful to your readers such as copies of patents or building and equipment leases may also be included.

You will want to include product or service collateral material to the extent that you have it available. If your product is small, include a sample. Product descriptions, screen shots of software, or service products should also be included. In short, incorporate anything that helps your reader understand the product or service and why your customer and market will be so interested.

If you are dealing with a bank or investor, ask for a list of expected addenda items. They will have a ready list of items they expect to be attached to the plan. Include any others items that help tell your story.

The following is a partial list of potential addenda items:

Owners Personal Documents
Personal Financial Statement
Owners Tax Returns
Resumes

Legal Documents
Real Estate Lease/Purchase Agreements
Equipment Lease/Purchase Agreements
Other Loan or Financing Agreements
Patents
Management Agreements
Manufacturing Agreements
Sales Representation Agreements
Non-Compete Agreements

Corporate Formation Documents

Articles of Organization/Incorporation
Operating Agreement/By-Laws
IRS Federal Employer Identification Number
Licenses & Permits

Product & Service Documents

Product Brochures
Published Articles and White Papers
Product Pictures
Product Specifications
Product Samples
Product MSDS Sheets
Product License Agreements
Health & Safety Information

Market Information

Market Studies
Competitor Marketing Information
Trade Journal & Magazine Articles
3rd Party Market Research

11 Summary

So that's it. Remember, the object of your business plan is not to impress your banker with a slick, hyper-produced document that you paid a small fortune to produce and print. A business plan is all about telling your story and convincing the reader to buy-in to your plan. When in doubt, remember the words of Leonardo Da Vinci, "Simplicity is the ultimate sophistication."

You can get your own copy of *Business Start-up 101: From Great Idea to Profit...Quick!* by visiting www.BusinessStartup101.com or Amazon.

ABOUT THE AUTHOR

Chris started what is now Blue Point Strategies, LLC, a business consultancy, in 1984. He works with business owners who are struggling with the business part of running a business. From start-ups to turnarounds, Chris works with owners of small businesses to develop strategies and systems so they can achieve the financial success that drove them into business in the first place. Blue Point Strategies offers workshops, classes, consulting, and one-on-one coaching to assist business owners in achieving their dreams.

Chris has a background in corporate finance and operations, having served in various direct capacities, including CFO of the nation's largest privately-held insulation and construction products distributor; credit manager for the U.S. division of a multinational construction products manufacturer; and director of a small plastics manufacturing business. He has over 27 years of successful experience managing start-ups and turnarounds of large and small businesses as well as financial analysis, budget formulation, strategic planning, team building, and risk management. Chris has managed small businesses, wrestled with unreasonable demands from banks, and struggled with cash flow to make payroll. He understands the needs of and demands on small business owners.

His consulting experiences range from advising individual clients on real estate financing and development activities to managing start-ups and turnarounds of small businesses. He also has advised on site selection and expansion activities for a major Japanese automaker and various Tier 1 auto suppliers.

Chris has served on local planning and zoning commissions and development authorities, giving him keen insight into dealing with local cities and towns to further his clients' needs. In addition to his consulting practice, Chris serves as a business coach for local entrepreneurial development centers, an instructor for an area technical college, and a keynote speaker. Blue Point Strategies offers workshops, classes, and one-on-one coaching to assist business owners in achieving their dreams.

Get Chris' complete start-up guide for starting a small business *Business Start-up 101: From Great Idea to Profit...Quick!* and complete start-up templates to download for free by visiting www.businessstartup101.com.

Blue Point Strategies, LLC
Huntsville, Alabama
www.BluePointStrategies.com

www.BusinessStartup101.com